Cool Swimming

A quick dip into cold water swimming and physical and mental well-being

SLSC
SOUTH LONDON
SWIMMING CLUB
TOOTING BEC LIDO

CONTENTS

Cool Swim	3
Introduction	4
Health Benefits of Cold Water Swimming	8
Summary of research results	8
Swimmers	10
Why they do it	13
Benefits to the body	15
Benefits to the mind	17
Upsides	19
Downsides	21
Academic Studies	22
Swim Safely	26
Cold Water Swimming; What you need to know	26
Ten Cool Tips	29
Cold Cures and Warm Hearts	31
Useful links	39
Author	40

Cool Swim

The frost in the grass and a bite in the air
The mist on the park, I'm going there
To the Lido, not sun-kissed yet not dark
But awakening with a brilliance
Turning leaves on water drifting

The old cast-iron turnstile rolls over with a squeak
To let us in and then goes back to sleep

Good morning … it's cold
Gold leaf and green leaf mingle
Mulched on pool and paving

Shed leaves, shed clothes and jump
Into the blue pool, to the bottom sinking
With a bump to bounce back breathing out
And stand up with a shout
"Brrrrrrreaghoah whoopy doo"
I feel the cold cutting through
The winter sleep

Rosie, seventy years old
Swims lovely bright and white in morning light
Young girl in Lido liquimelting

And in the autumn as we grow old
We too like leaves can turn to gold
Coming in then going out
Against the turnstile's turnabout

Introduction

Cool Swimming looks at the relationship between cold water swimming and general well-being. It presents the results of research with over 300 participants in the UK Cold Water Swimming Championships 2013. There is also an overview of current academic research, a history of cold water therapy and tips on swimming safely.

Members of South London Swimming Club have been swimming year round since soon after Tooting Bec Lido opened in 1906. Because there used to be so many older swimmers, the belief grew that cold water was the key to a longer and healthier life. Then someone pointed out that only survivors live to tell the story and if you swim during winter you probably have a pretty strong constitution.

But even in Roman times, they were talking about the health benefits of a cold dip. We reprint the article *Cold Cures and Warm Hearts* (page 31) from the March 2002 edition of Positive Health Magazine. It sketches out the history of cold water therapy and highlights some of the reported benefits for conditions ranging from multiple sclerosis through to arthritis and the common cold.

In recent times, a number of formal academic research reports have also identified positive outcomes from cold water swimming (Academic Studies page 22). A study in Finland found that winter swimming in moderation seems to improve general well-being. Another in Germany suggests it can help create more 'brown fat' which makes it easier for the body to burn off 'body fat deposits' and reduce risk of heart disease.

But until recently no-one had really asked the swimmers. As founders and organisers of the biennial UK Cold Water Swimming Championships, South London Swimming Club (SLSC) decided to dive in and poll competitors on the whys and wherefores. Some 300 participants at the 2013 championships took part. Their views provide an interesting addition to the limited body of writing on this subject.

One of those surveyed, described the practice of cold water swimming as an 'oddball' pursuit. It certainly used to be but gradually it seems to be entering the mainstream. An increased interest in swimming, triathlon and the elemental pleasure of 'wild swimming', allied to the capability to share this enthusiasm with others via social media, is driving steady growth in cold water swimming.

This is a big change from when I first started swimming at Tooting Bec in the middle of the 1980s. Lidos were being closed and only a few hardy souls swam through the winter.

Not surprising given that there seemed no sense in, or demand for, keeping an unheated pool open during the winter. Even in summer, people were wary of the cold water.

Then the Club had maybe 60 members and had to fight a hard campaign to keep the Lido open year round. The great worry was that if it closed during the winter it might never open again. The pool was built by the unemployed of Wandsworth and the goal of the campaign was to maintain the tradition of winter swimming at the Lido and in doing so to preserve the legacy of these working men for future generations.

The campaign succeeded and out of it evolved a community partnership with the local council and pool operators that has enabled Tooting Bec Lido and the South London Swimming Club to go from strength to strength. And underpinning the long term sustainability is the fact that from the start, the campaign was not just about one Lido but all Lidos and the promotion of outdoor swimming.

Now some 30 years on, over 600 swimmers take part in the over-subscribed biennial UK Cold Water Swimming Championships. And Club membership is well over 1,300 members and growing.

Not all of them swim through winter but the love of winter and the practice of cold water swimming has indeed spread throughout the land with more outdoor pools staying open during the winter.

And long may this trend continue! It's cool swimming outdoors in autumn, winter and spring. Mind, body and spirit seem to benefit from being in touch with elements in a pure and uncompromising way. Zen Master Unmon could have been speaking for winter swimmers when he said, 'every day is a good day!'

But read on and hear what the practitioners themselves have to say about cold water swimming and well-being. And if you like what you learn, go for a swim in the great outdoors. We've included a few tips on how to stay safe.

Jonathan Buckley

Health Benefits of Cold Water Swimming

Summary of Findings

Some 304 swimmers completed the online survey in the period November-December 2013. About 80% were over the age of 40 years, with slightly more women than men taking part. Most (87%) had swum in freezing conditions. Half swam two to three times a week, one in ten swam every day and around a third, swam 'now and then'.

The majority swam at Tooting Bec Lido. Others took their cold water swimming where they could; up and down the country and overseas in Ireland, the USA, Canada, Latvia and many other countries. It seems that cold water swimmers will do it wherever they can: in lakes, seas, dams, rivers, lochs, lidos and ponds. Why do they do it?

It makes me feel alive and gives me a buzz … The challenge and the feel good factor afterwards … Love the weather elements

To experience nature in a different way ... To get out of the comfort zone and push myself a bit ... Love the water, nature, outdoors, community and conviviality

It's a mind over matter thing and you feel great afterwards ... I like to meet the elements in winter rather than staying cocooned

Three quarters believed that cold water swimming is addictive and that it improves circulation and the immune system. Half were pretty much convinced that it improved metabolism and complexion. And one in four believed that it burns up fat and improves libido; 'almost as good as an orgasm!'

Most agreed that cold water swimming alleviates depression. In fact the consensus was that the practice connects them with the natural world and people from all walks of life. It boosts self-confidence and resilience, provides great camaraderie and encourages an alternative view of life.

Swimmers

Some 304 people completed the survey by the last day in 2012. Most swam without a wetsuit in temperatures ranging from freezing 0°C to 17°C. The majority were from the UK but our poll also featured those who swam in South Africa, Latvia, Canada, Australia, Czech Republic, Slovakia and the USA.

Most respondents were over 40 years of age. Two thirds were aged between 40-59 years of age. Of the remainder, 19% were aged between 17-39 years, 11% were over 60 and one was 16 or younger. There were slightly more women (55%) than men (45%). Many had been attracted to cold water swimming in the last five years.

How long have you been a cold water swimmer?

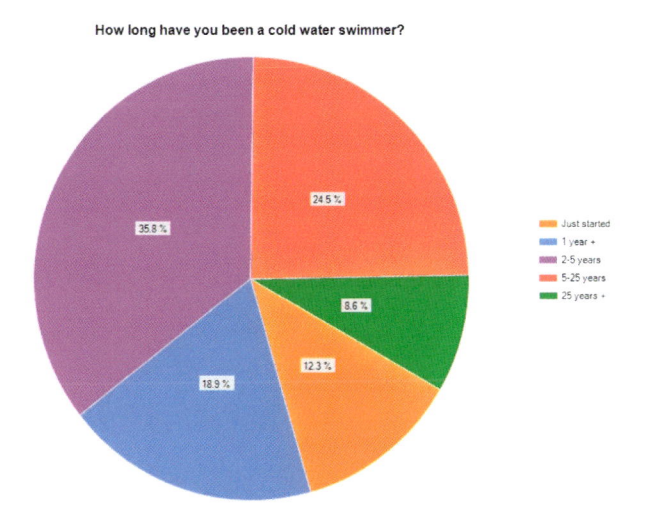

- Just started: 12.3%
- 1 year +: 18.9%
- 2-5 years: 35.8%
- 5-25 years: 24.5%
- 25 years +: 8.6%

Most of the swimmers had swum in freezing temperatures. Some 14% swam every day; 55% a couple of times a week; and 32% now and then. And they did this in lidos, the sea, lochs, rivers, marinas, dams, lakes, ponds, tarns, waterfalls, dykes, canals, harbours, tidal pools, in fact 'anywhere' they could!

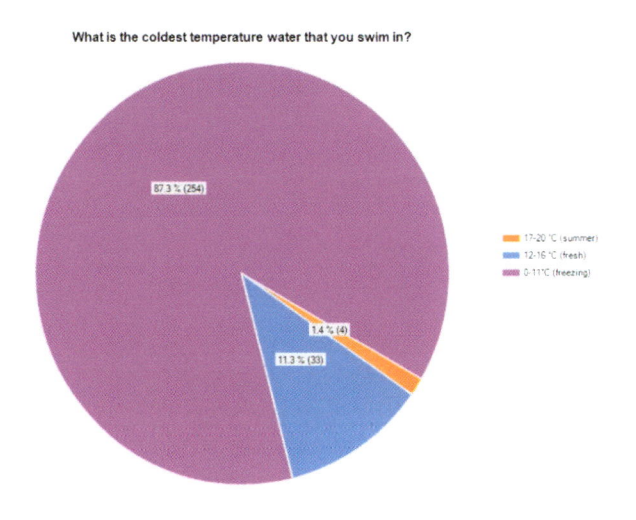

What is the coldest temperature water that you swim in?

- 17-20 °C (summer): 1.4% (4)
- 12-16 °C (fresh): 11.3% (33)
- 0-11°C (freezing): 87.3% (254)

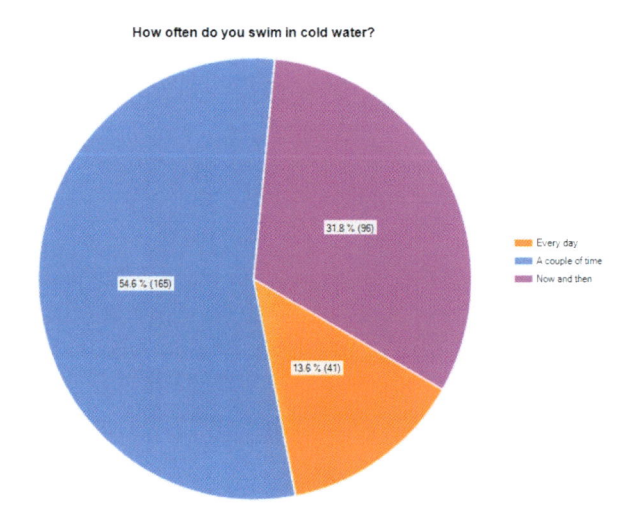

How often do you swim in cold water?

- Every day: 13.6 % (41)
- A couple of time: 54.6 % (165)
- Now and then: 31.8 % (96)

Why they do it

The reasons for swimming in cold water were varied. Some were training to swim the Channel while others just wanted to be healthy and engage with nature and the elements. There was a lot about increasing confidence, fun and stress busting, even a sense of achievement and slight insanity.

The cold, the water, the light, the air, the sauna, the camaraderie, and the cake …

The fun of it … the high … because if you swim wild the rest of the year it is just a natural extension or challenge … as part of festive swims …. To celebrate being alive

Love the sensation, the sense of freedom and being at one with the elements … Makes all the blues go away and cures my eczema

Well-being which I put down partly to the effects of cold water and partly to the friendship and camaraderie of my fellow cold water swimmers - a very supportive and non-judgemental community

Part of being a retired playboy ... I enjoy the challenge of entering the water and the mental state you have to adopt to overcome the initial discomfort. I leave the pool exhilarated and clear-headed

Benefits to the body

Almost everyone said the practice of cold water swimming is quite an addictive high. Three quarters agreed that it strengthens the immune system and improves circulation while more than half agreed that it increases metabolism (59%) and improves the complexion (55%). Two in five agreed that cold water swimming burns up fat so you lose weight.

Over a quarter agreed that cold water swimming is almost as good as an orgasm and a similar number agreed that it enhances libido. But only 7% agreed that the practice improves fertility. That said no-one actively disagreed – 82% of respondents didn't know. Finally, some 15% agreed that it can stop the build-up of cellulite.

To what extent do you agree with these statements about the benefits to the body of regular, outdoor, cold water swimming:

- Strengthens the immune system
- Delivers a 'high' that is quite addictive
- Is almost as good as an orgasm
- Improves circulation
- Improves the complexion
- Stops the build-up of cellulite
- Enhances sexual libido
- Improves fertility
- Increases metabolism
- Burns up fat so you lose weight

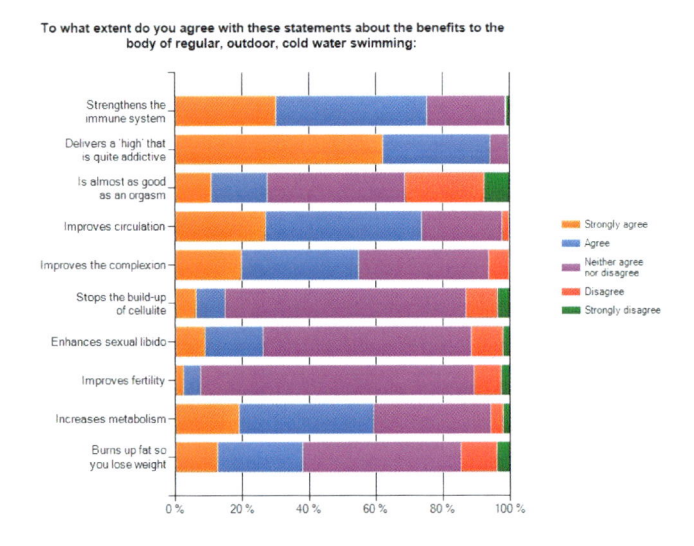

Legend: Strongly agree / Agree / Neither agree nor disagree / Disagree / Strongly disagree

Clarifies thinking and improves mood ... Alleviates back pain ... Believe it a great preventative for heart conditions ... Out of thinking and into sensual

Improves injuries (cold alleviates swelling) ... Makes my breasts pert ... Alleviates joint pain ... Sleep better!

Improves arthritis in my thumbs from my work

Assists childbirth: I swam in the Lido while in early labour and had a very easy and quick birth

Exposes body to sunlight during winter months, helping to replenish store of Vitamin D which in turn strengthens the immune system

Benefits to the mind

Everyone agreed that cold water swimming puts them in touch with the natural world and most (91%) felt that getting in to cold water was 'better than banging your head against a brick wall'.

A similar number agreed that one of the great pleasures and benefits was the camaraderie that exists between cold water swimmers and the variety of people from all walks of life that do it. There was fairly unanimous agreement that it boosts self-confidence and resilience (89%), encourages an alternative view of life (86%), and alleviates depression (86%).

To what extent do you agree with the following statements on the benefits to the mind of regular, outdoor, cold water swimming:

- Alleviates depression
- Connects you with the natural world
- Connect with people from all walks of life
- Boosts self confidence and resilience
- Offers a great sense of camaraderie
- Encourages an alternative view of life
- Is better than banging your head against a brick wall

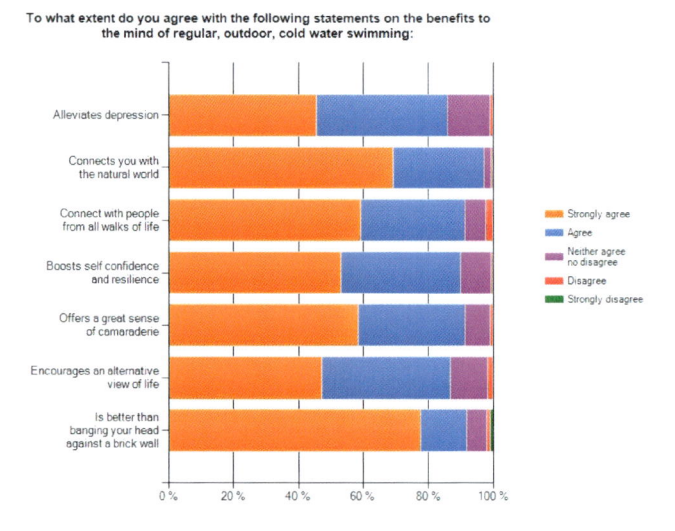

Legend: Strongly agree, Agree, Neither agree no disagree, Disagree, Strongly disagree

Sense of achievement ... Helps you live in the moment ... Heightens senses especially smell

Gives me a positive view of my body despite having some significant missing parts

Age is not known, we are all equal in water ... Is calming and brings concerns and pressures into perspective

After doing it nothing in your day can be so bad ... Helps effects of being broken down by age and sex

Gives a focus point for those who are not working

Alleviates SAD

Upside

Happiness ... My office is overheated; a few minutes pre-cooling in 2 degrees water set me up nicely for a comfortable day

Puts a huge smile on my face ... Knowledge that you can take your body further than one would have thought possible

At peace with the world ... Sense of freedom ... Spend less on my heating bill ... Great for self-confidence ... Solitude

The light is pretty fantastic and lifts my mood ... Eases back pains and headaches ... I'm epileptic and it calms my brain

Ability to succeed at a sport without being athletic ... Puts the rest of life in perspective

Sense of pride - not everyone can or wants to swim in cold water but typically they are in awe of people who do

Sense of being in a group of quite special people ... I believe shivering improves my muscle definition - people pay lots of money to cause the same 'spasming' by electric current

Never had a cold since I started ... It's very good for MS, symptoms are relieved after cold water swimming - for a few hours at least

Self-discipline: it makes everything else seem easy ... Heals micro tears in the muscles

Downside

Without a sauna it can take a while to warm up; and sometimes during this your brain is not your best ally ... Below 2°C numbness and tingling in fingers can result and last a few months

Overdoing it and then having a hot shower afterwards can make you feel unwell - better to towel dry and warm up with hot drink ... Risk of hypothermia ... Walking without shoes from the steps to the changing room post swim ... Too cold to stay in long

Warming up can take longer than the swim ... A cold wind blowing up your 'Robie' ... Chilblains ... Loss of feeling in fingers and toes ... Possibility of amnesia, unconsciousness, and cardiac arrest

That would be a question for my wife... Soggy socks and chilly boobs ... Getting cold inside your kidneys ... Sometimes worsens my tinnitus ... Aggravates Reynaud's disease ... Divorce ... Wife bans me from bed

Academic Studies

A number of academic studies have identified benefits from cold water swimming. A study in Finland found that it in moderation it seems to improve general well-being. Separate studies in Germany suggest it also enhances the body's ability to resist oxidative stress and the damaging effects of ROS (reactive oxygen species) and helps create more brown fat, thereby allowing bodies to burn off excess body fat deposits and reduce risk of heart disease.

General well-being

The study 'Winter swimming improves general well-being' was conducted with 36 winter swimmers and 23 controls. Objective ratings were made using profile of mood states such as tension, fatigue, confusion, vigour and depression. Subjective factors were also measured covering mood, memory, alertness, sleep quality, and somatic symptoms

The study results suggest a significant decrease in tension, fatigue, memory and mood negative state points. After four months the winter swimmers were more energetic, active and brisk than controls. Vigour activity scores were significantly higher and there was also reported pain relief amongst suffers from rheumatism, fibromyalgia and asthma.

The study was published in *The International Journal of Circumpolar Health 63:2 2004*. The authors were Pirkko Huttunen, Department of Forensic Medicine, University of Oulu, Leena Kokko, Winter Swimming Centre of Kajaani, Virpi Ylijukuri, Medivire Occupational Services, Oulu, Finland.

Antioxidative protection

In the 1998 paper 'Improved antioxidative protection in winter swimmers', Dr T. Grune of the Medical Faculty of Humboldt University reports on an investigation to find out whether the repeated oxidative stress in winter swimmers results in improved antioxidative adaptation.

Oxidative stress is when the body has to deal with an abnormal level of reactive oxygen species (ROS), such as the free radicals or non-radicals. These cause 'oxidative damage' to certain molecules with consequential injury to cells or tissue. The way to remove or neutralize ROS is with antioxidants.

Using winter swimmers as the model for 'whole-body cold-exposure-induced oxidative stress', the team found that antioxidative protection was improved through preconditioning with repeated mild oxidative stress.

Changes in uric acid and glutathione levels during ice-bathing suggest that the intensive voluntary short-term cold exposure of winter swimming produces oxidative stress that encourages oxidative adaption and thereby improves the body's ability to resist the damaging effects of ROS.

http://qjmed.oxfordjournals.org/content/92/4/193.full

Triglyceride clearance

An article in the *Daily Telegraph* of 13 February 2011 – 'A dose of the cold could help weight-loss and reduce heart disease' - reported how researchers at the University Medical Centre Hamburg-Eppendorf, found that keeping mice at temperatures of around 39.2°F (4°C) increased the ability of the animal's brown fat to burn off these molecules and reduced levels of body fat.

Dr Bartelt and his colleagues, whose research is published in the scientific journal *Nature Medicine*, now believe that regularly exposing human patients to cold conditions could help create more brown fat, allowing their bodies to burn off excess body fat deposits and reduce their risk of heart disease.

"If one is able to stimulate brown fat development in humans by pharmacological or biological approaches, elevated blood lipids and obesity are at the top of the list of diseases that can be cured using brown fat."

Improving surgical outcomes

In his paper 'Extreme preconditioning: cold adaptation through sea swimming as a means to improve surgical outcomes', Mark Harper of Brighton Anaesthetic

Research Forum at the Royal Sussex County Hospital draws parallels between the surgical stress response and the response to cold exposure and hypothesises how a programme of sea bathing may be used to enhance postoperative recovery and reduce preoperative complications.

Explaining the inspiration for this approach, he notes that the practice of sea bathing for its health benefits was popularised by Richard Russell in Regency Brighton during the 18th Century. Although the cures he claimed may seem a little far-fetched today, as with many historical remedies, there is much to be gained from revisiting such theories in the light of modern medical research.

http://www.ncbi.nlm.nih.gov/pubmed/22305336

Swim Safely

Cold Water Swimming – What you need to know

Cold dips are exhilarating but to enjoy them safely we need to be aware of the common conditions that cold water swimmers face. So here is an edited version of South London Swimming Club's guide, *Cold Water Swimming - What you need to know.*

Cold Shock

Acclimatise yourself to cold water swimming gradually, over a period of weeks, and don't just jump in or do a long swim the first time. Sudden immersion in very cold water (below 15 °C) can be dangerous if you are not used to it. It may lead to thermal shock and hypothermia.

Sudden cold water in the mouth sets off a reflex that makes you feel breathless, and some people panic with that feeling. The ribcage contracts, which makes many swimmers feel they can't breathe. Exhale and the next breath will come in naturally.

Hypothermia

Cold water cools down the body 25 times faster than cold air does. Any physical activity only increases the body's heat loss. It causes muscle rigidity and dangerous loss of manual dexterity. The obvious precaution is to get out of the water before you start to feel cold.

Physical weakness occurs at body temperature of about 35 °C. Mental ability also deteriorates at this point. Unconsciousness occurs when the body's core temperature falls below 30 °C. The body shuts down when the core temperature is about 27 °C. If this occurs in the water you will drown.

One of the dangers of hypothermia is that the swimmer often does not realise that it is setting in. If you feel weak, light-headed or woozy, or think that the water feels comfortable, it's time to get out. If you do feel ill, faint, or unwell, wrap up quickly and alert a lifeguard or another swimmer.

Fainting

When the body is surrounded by warm air or water in a sauna or shower the blood vessels on the surface relax, allowing heat loss from the surface. This has two consequences; firstly, if your core is still cold, you will take longer to warm up and may get colder.

Secondly, blood pressure drops. This is more pronounced in the shower than in the sauna, but you may not notice till you get up and then suddenly the pressure in the circulation is too low and insufficient for the brain. It recovers quickly in healthy people, but does cause fainting.

If you get too cold, avoid the temptation of using the hot shower or sauna to warm up. Wrap up well instead.

Asthma and Heart

Immersion in cold water dangerously increases the chance of fatal cardiac arrhythmia (irregular heart beat). Asthma is also made worse by cold conditions. Always make sure you have your inhaler or other treatment nearby, and follow any medically prescribed guidelines.

Cold Urticaria

'Cold hives' is an allergy where red welts form on the skin after exposure to the cold. They are usually itchy and often the hands and feet are affected. Hives vary in size from about the size of a pencil eraser to as big as a fifty pence piece or larger. If you have the symptoms check with your GP.

Ten Tips for Cool Swimming

1. If you have never swum in cold water before, let an experienced cold water swimmer or one of the lifeguards know. They can advise and make sure your first swim is a happy one.

2. Wear a swimming hat or two during the winter months as this will help you retain heat.

3. Bring plenty of warm clothing with you, including a hat and warm socks and change into them as soon as you get out of the pool.

4. Acclimatise yourself to cold water over a period of weeks. Maybe that means just getting in for a quick dip at first. Keep moving when in the water and extend your swim gradually. If you feel dizzy when you get out you've probably stayed in too long.

5. Ask for help if you feel very cold, ill, woozy, or disorientated. Far better to recognise the signs that

something is wrong and say something, rather than attempt to battle through it alone.

6. Watch out for others. If you think someone has overdone it stay with them and make sure they are OK. Don't assume someone else will deal with the situation and remember that people who are hypothermic may not realise something is wrong.

7. Everyone is different so learn to recognise your limits. In winter many swimmers only swim a width or two. There are no prizes for swimming more lengths than anybody else over winter.

8. Warm up gently. Standing under a hot shower or sitting in the sauna for a long time can cause fainting. Have a quick shower and then wrap up warmly.

9. Shivering is the body's natural mechanism for warming up. If you shiver for a while then you are warming up but if it goes on you have stayed in too long. Also be aware that someone suffering from hypothermia will not normally be shivering.

10. Consult your GP if you suffer from heart disease, asthma, lung conditions or other medical conditions that might be affected by exposure to cold water. And if you are pregnant, do not swim without consulting your GP first.

Cold Cures and Warm Hearts*

Cold baths are usually associated with punishment or passion killing but for some people they hold the secret to a happy and healthy life. Jonathan Buckley explains.

There's a band of eccentrics who swim all the year round at Tooting Bec Lido. They start arriving at dawn to bear witness to the new day. Plunging into icy water midst the sound of birdsong, they emerge after a few strokes or indeed several lengths, invigorated and ready to face whatever the world may throw at them. From Lords to window cleaners, young and old, male and female, all of them will tell you in their own particular way that "it does you good", that "you won't get any colds" (but of course you do) and that "it is the secret to a long and happy life".

And they are not alone; like-minded souls can be found swimming at Hampstead Ponds, the Serpentine and Hampton and then further afield in the UK, and overseas in Finland, Russia and the USA. Cold water seems to supercharge the system, improving breathing and muscle tone and decreasing fatigue. Some connoisseurs even attribute improved thyroid function and skin tone together with relief from constipation, to a five-minute dip!

The practice of bathing in cold water can be traced back to the first century BC, when the Romans adopted cold-water baths as a cure for stomach problems and headaches. Emperor Augustus (27 BC - 14 BC) made the practice a national passion after his physician Antonius Musa recommended a cold mineral bath as a cure for an abscessed liver. When Augustus survived the painful ailment, Musa became rich, and his cure fashionable.

Many of the swimmers at Tooting Bec Lido share the view that cold is better than warm. In the 1980s, many opposed a plan to heat the pool, as they do at Hampton Pool in West London, not on the grounds of expense, which would be considerable, but because it somehow compromised the essence of the practice and the Lido's position as a 'natural' haven in the heart of the city.

The early morning swim, in what has been described as 'Europe's largest refrigerated pool', can be likened to a kind of pagan practice; a particularly vigorous meditation on the elements of each new day. There's the temperature to consider - up or down? How does the water feel? Soft and silky after the rain, or sticky as Velcro when the frost has bitten?

Preparing to enter the water, the mind focuses on the here and now. Yesterday's cares, and the trials to come, dissolve in the play of light on water and the shock of entering it. Eighty-year old 'Doctor Andy' walks with crutches following a failed hip replacement. He jokingly describes his swim as a form of penance: "It gives me the right to live another day. I used to bang my head against a brick wall, this is much better."

Developing Tolerance

Most of the year-round swimmers believe that a dip in the Lido makes them better able to cope with the stress of modern-day urban living, and more resilient to cold weather. The latter has a number of precedents which pop up in a fascinating book called *Life at the Extremes - The Science of Survival* by Frances Ashcroft.

In a chapter entitled 'Life in the Cold', the author cites the story of Scott's 1911 expedition to the South Pole which recounts how expedition member Birdie HG Bowers slept soundly in temperatures below -20 °C without the eiderdown lining of his sleeping bag, while his companion suffered extreme shivering. He never suffered from frostbite and every morning stripped naked in the freezing Antarctic air to douse himself with buckets of icy water and slush.

Other hardened types cited in the chapter include: the Yaga Indians of Tierra del Fuego who lived through the snow and ice of Patagonian winters without any clothing (but fires); and Australian Aborigines and Kalahari tribesmen who sleep naked in a windbreak, despite night temperatures of below freezing.

Ashcroft reports that controlled experiments have confirmed the belief that the body does indeed adapt to the cold. Immersing nude volunteers in water at 15 °C for 30 to 60 minutes over several weeks resulted in greater tolerance and less discomfort when they were subsequently exposed to Arctic conditions.

We 21st-century urban dwellers don't need that level of physical endurance but we might benefit from the sense of well-being that goes with it. Cold water is known to stimulate the hypothalamus and release endorphins, thereby putting the 'feel good' back into everyday living.

The experts on this are the Finns. Half a million of the 5.5 million inhabitants went ice swimming and 80,000 did it at least once a week last year. They have a bestselling manual on the practice of 'ice swimming' called *Ice Ecstasy*. It is written by journalist Pasi Heikura, anthropologist Taina Kinnunen and forensic medical specialist Pirkko Huttenen.

Extracting the Benefits

But it's not just the 'feel good' that cold water creates. Claims have also been made for the therapeutic effect of cold bathing on specific conditions. Reports suggest that ME (myalgic encephalomyelitis) sufferers may benefit from daily cold baths which seem to stimulate and 'kick start' the hormonal immune system (www.womannova.com).

The website www.healthlibrary.com reports that those suffering from painful periods may find relief in a programme of cold hip baths between periods (to increase the tone of the ovaries) and then hot hip baths on alternate nights in the week before starting.

Cold water has also been shown to be a performance enhancer. US swimming champion Ron Karnaugh reports how the former East Germans pioneered a training technique called shrinkage, which enables you to train harder and more often without sore or stiff muscles.

During a workout, muscles can fill with lactic acid, which creates the 'burn' sensation. A hot shower after training causes small blood vessels to expand and trap blood and waste material in the muscles causing stiff and tender muscles the next day. Cold water reverses this process, resulting in loose, pain-free muscles that are ready for the next day's work-out.

And researchers at Charles Sturt University in Australia have discovered that endurance athletes competing in warm climates can improve their performance by taking cold baths before events. The internal body temperature is reduced by sitting in a cold bath for about an hour prior to performing. Over a 30-minute run, the athletes averaged 300 metres more than they achieved without cooling.

Dealing with the Cold

The body reacts to cooling by sucking all the warm blood back into the core of the body to nourish and protect vital organs. When the extremities begin to suffer from the lack of circulation, the blood vessels dilate and the blood comes rushing back to prevent damage to the skin.

This explains why swimmers can emerge as red as a beetroot from a particularly long, cold swim. The truth is, nothing gets the heart pumping quite like a cold dip (except perhaps for sex!). Just look at those beatific smiles after a swim!

But think twice before throwing caution, and clothes, to the winds. Jumping in to very cold water can take your breath away and make the heart skip a beat. Winter swimmers tend to splash themselves with water before going in and often enter the water slowly (a particularly exquisite form of torture).

And once you get over the shock, cold water can become disarmingly comfortable. Water saps body heat much faster than air, and if you stay in too long this can lead to the early stages of hypothermia.

If the body's core temperature falls by just 1 °C, reactions are slowed and judgement impaired; so it is important to be moderate in your winter swimming habits and wear a bathing cap. You lose most of your body heat through the head and the nerve endings on the scalp are very sensitive, so putting your head under in icy water can be quite painful, like putting your head in a vice and tightening it.

Warming the Heart

But, if one is sensible, the cold dip is the perfect antidote to our increasingly frenetic and mechanized lifestyle. And it's not just about the body but also about the community that exists around these 'bathing ponds', as Tooting Bec Lido was originally described.

Every Sunday, members of the South London Swimming Club, who are proud that they 'swim for fun not for medals', meet for a handicap race. This practice has been going since 1908 and is remarkable for the way that the Right Honourable Handicapper manipulates start times so that the fastest and the slowest touch the end together.

After the race there is coffee and home-made cakes and a lot of leg-pulling. On winter days and birthdays, there's also a shot of something a bit stronger. For them, the early morning swim is not just a cure for the common cold, it's also the way to a warm heart!

(c) Jonathan Buckley

* A slightly longer version of this article was published in *Positive Health Magazine*, March 2002.

Useful links

This is a selection of blogs and websites for cool swimmers. Just put the name + swimming into google to follow up.

- Devon Dispatches
- Do You Swim Here Often
- Lone Swimmer
- Miss Adventures
- Musings of an Aquatic Ape
- Open Water Swimming
- Outdoor Swimming Society
- Quick Dip – Pictures from Tooting Bec Lido
- River Access Campaign
- Sandy Cove Swimmers
- South London Swimming Club
- Swimming Round London
- The Long Swim
- The Next Challenge
- Unusual Love Affair with London
- Vivienne Rickman
- Wild Woman Swimming

Author

Jonathan Buckley discovered Tooting Bec Lido in the 1980s and has been swimming there ever since. The enjoyment comes from engaging with the elements and the companionship of other swimmers throughout the year. He is a member of South London Swimming Club and when he is not down at the Lido, he plays guitar and works as a writer and market communications consultant. http://jpdbuckley.co.uk

Printed in Great Britain
by Amazon